Year 2

Excellence in Problem Solving Mathematics

Hilary Koll and Steve Mills

RISING STARS

Rising Stars UK Ltd.

7 Hatchers Mews, Bermondsey Street, London, SE1 3GS

www.risingstars-uk.com

Every effort has been made to trace copyright holders and obtain their permission for the use of copyright materials. The authors and publisher will gladly receive information enabling them to rectify any error or omission in subsequent editions.

All facts are correct at time of going to press.

Published 2010
Reprinted 2012

Authors: Hilary Koll and Steve Mills
Design and typesetting: Sally Boothroyd
Editorial: Bruce Nicholson, Ruth Burns
Artwork: Sally Boothroyd, Michael Emmerson, David Woodroffe
Cover Design: Words and Pictures
Photo acknowledgements
p.13 *lottery balls* © Simon Askham/iStockphoto; **p.17** *banana* © Kutay Tanir/iStockphoto, *watermelon* © Paul George Bodea/iStockphoto, *apricot* © S Mistika/iStockphoto, *grapefruit* © Edd Westmacott/iStockphoto, *grape* © OnlyLight/iStockphoto; p.27 *parking sign* © Jonathan Ling/iStockphoto

British Library Cataloguing in Publication Data.
A CIP record for this book is available from the British Library.

ISBN: 978-1-84680-760-2

Printed by Craft Print International Ltd, Singapore.

Contents

	Using and applying mathematics					Counting and understanding number					Knowing and using number facts			
	Solve problems involving addition, subtraction, multiplication or division in contexts of numbers, measures or pounds and pence	Identify and record the information or calculation needed to solve a puzzle or problem; carry out the steps or calculations and check the solution in the context of the problem	Follow a line of enquiry; answer questions by choosing and using suitable equipment and selecting, organising and presenting information in lists, tables and simple diagrams	Describe patterns and relationships involving numbers or shapes, make predictions and test these with examples	Present solutions to puzzles and problems in an organised way; explain decisions, methods and results in pictorial, spoken or written form, using mathematical language and number sentences	Read and write two- and three-digit numbers in figures and words; describe and extend number sequences and recognise odd and even numbers	Count up to 100 objects by grouping them and counting in tens, fives or twos; explain what each digit in a two-digit number represents, including numbers where 0 is a place holder; partition two-digit numbers in different ways, including into multiples of 10 and one	Order two-digit numbers and position them on a number line; use the greater than (>) and less than (<) signs	Estimate a number of objects; round two-digit numbers to the nearest 10	Find one half, one quarter and three quarters of shapes and sets of objects	Derive and recall all addition and subtraction facts for each number to at least 10, all pairs with totals to 20 and all pairs of multiples of 10 with totals up to 100	Understand that halving is the inverse of doubling and derive and recall doubles of all numbers to 20, and the corresponding halves	Derive and recall multiplication facts for the 2, 5 and 10 times-tables and the related division facts; recognise multiples of 2, 5 and 10	Use knowledge of number facts and operations to estimate and check answers to calculations
Practical problems	✔	✔		✔	✔						✔			
Patterns and sequences	✔	✔		✔	✔	✔	✔							
Addition and subtraction	✔	✔		✔	✔						✔			✔
Doubling and halving	✔	✔		✔	✔							✔	✔	✔
Multiplication and division	✔	✔		✔	✔							✔	✔	✔
Mixed calculations	✔	✔		✔	✔						✔	✔	✔	✔
Fractions	✔	✔		✔	✔					✔		✔		✔
Place value and ordering	✔	✔		✔	✔	✔	✔	✔					✔	
Money	✔	✔		✔	✔		✔				✔	✔	✔	
Number lines	✔	✔		✔	✔		✔	✔						
Measures – length	✔	✔		✔	✔									
Measures – capacity	✔	✔		✔	✔									
Measures – mass	✔	✔		✔	✔									
Time	✔	✔		✔	✔									
2-D and 3-D shapes	✔	✔		✔	✔									
Position and direction	✔	✔		✔	✔									
Tables	✔	✔	✔	✔	✔									
Graphs, charts and diagrams	✔	✔	✔	✔	✔									

	Calculating — Add or subtract mentally a one-digit number, or a multiple of 10, to or from any two-digit number; use practical and informal written methods to add and subtract two-digit numbers	Understand that subtraction is the inverse of addition and vice versa and use this to derive and record related addition and subtraction number sentences	Represent repeated addition and arrays as multiplication, and sharing and repeated subtraction (grouping) as division; use practical and informal written methods and related vocabulary to support multiplication and division, including calculations with remainders	Use the symbols +, −, ×, ÷ and = to record and interpret number sentences involving all four operations; calculate the value of an unknown in a number sentence, e.g. $\square \div 2 = 6$, $30-\square = 24$	Understanding shape — Visualise common 2-D shapes and 3-D solids; identify shapes from pictures of them in different positions and orientations; sort, make and describe shapes, referring to their properties	Identify reflective symmetry in patterns and 2-D shapes and draw lines of symmetry in shapes	Follow and give instructions involving position, direction and movement	Recognise and use whole, half and quarter turns, both clockwise and anticlockwise; know that a right angle represents a quarter turn	Measuring — Estimate, compare and measure lengths, weights and capacities, choosing and using standard units (m, cm, kg, litre) and suitable measuring instruments	Read the numbered divisions on a scale, and interpret the divisions between them, e.g. on a scale from 0 to 25 with intervals of 1 shown, but only the divisions 0, 5, 10, 15 and 20 numbered; use a ruler to draw and measure lines to the nearest centimetre	Use units of time (seconds, minutes, hours, days) and know the relationships between them; read the time to the quarter hour; identify time intervals, including those that cross the hour	Handling data — Answer a question by collecting and recording data in lists and tables; represent the data as block graphs or pictograms to show results; use ICT to organise and present data	Use lists, tables and diagrams to sort objects; explain choices using appropriate language, including *not*
Practical problems	✔				✔								
Patterns and sequences	✔	✔											
Addition and subtraction	✔	✔	✔	✔									
Doubling and halving				✔									
Multiplication and division			✔	✔									
Mixed calculations	✔	✔	✔	✔									
Fractions													
Place value and ordering													
Money	✔	✔	✔	✔									
Number lines										✔			
Measures – length									✔	✔			
Measures – capacity									✔	✔			
Measures – mass									✔	✔			
Time											✔		
2-D and 3-D shapes					✔	✔							
Position and direction							✔	✔					
Tables												✔	✔
Graphs, charts and diagrams												✔	✔

How to use this book

This book is designed to help you use your mathematical skills to solve a range of problems, many of which are written in words rather than figures.

Rather than giving a calculation like:

$$4 \times 6 = \boxed{}$$

a word problem might be something like:

If I have 4 six-packs of cola, how many cans of cola do I have in total?

The answer is the same, but you need to think about it a bit more and remember to answer by writing or saying: *I have 24 cans of cola in total.*

The example problem

The flow chart takes you through an example problem step-by-step. This is important when answering word problems as it helps you to order your thoughts, do each part of the problem in the right order and check your work!

Every problem has the same five steps:

READ the question, then read it again

DECIDE your operations and units

APPROXIMATE your answer

CALCULATE

CHECK your answer

We can remember this by using this mnemonic:

Rain

Drops

Are

Crystal

Clear

The introduction

This section of each page gives you an idea of the sort of problems you are likely to see and helps you to understand what maths you need to use.

Fractions

Some questions are about finding halves and quarters of shapes, numbers or sets of objects.

Ahmed cuts three pizzas into quarters. He shares the pieces equally between six people. How many pieces of pizza does each person get?

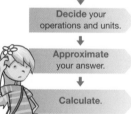

Read the question, now read it again.

↓

Decide your operations and units.

↓

Approximate your answer.

↓

Calculate.

↓

Check.

Read slowly and carefully. What are the important numbers?

Each pizza is cut into 4 slices (quarters). There are 3 pizzas. I must then share them between 6 people.

If there are 6 people and 3 pizzas they should each get about half a pizza, which is two of the quarter slices.

$3 \times 4 = 12$ and $12 \div 6 = 2$ so the answer must be 2 pieces each.

6×2 slices = 12 slices. Each slice is a quarter, 12 slices is 3 whole pizzas, so I am correct!

Hints and tips

- A half ($\frac{1}{2}$) means something has been split into two equal parts.
- A quarter ($\frac{1}{4}$) means it has been split into four equal parts.

22

Hints and tips

The Hints and tips section gives you useful ideas for completing the problems on the opposite page. These are the things you need to remember if you are doing a quiz or test.

The questions

The questions get harder as you go down the page.

- Section 1 questions are fairly straightforward and help you to practise your skills.

- Section 2 questions are a bit harder. They will help you to remember all the key points.

FRACTIONS

Questions

1 a) A basket holds 12 slices of garlic bread. Half of them are eaten. How many are not eaten?

b) There are eight olives on Li's pizza. Li eats one-quarter of them. How many olives does she leave?

c) Five pizzas are cut into quarters. How many quarters are there altogether?

2 a) A large pizza is cut into 20 slices. Three-quarters of the slices have ham on and one-quarter of the slices do not have ham on them. How many slices have ham on them?

b) Normally, a large pizza costs £9 and a small costs £6. But all pizzas are now half price. How much will it cost for 2 large pizzas and a small pizza in the sale?

CHALLENGE

Is each of these statements **True** or **False**?
- Half of one half is a quarter.
- One-quarter and three-quarters together make one whole.
- Two-quarters and one-half together make one whole.
- Four-quarters together make two wholes.

Challenge

The Challenge is really tough and sometimes involves making up games and your own questions.

Explore

Write a short report about how halves and quarters are used when telling the time. Include some questions and answers like this one: *What time is three-quarters of an hour after seven fifteen?*

23

Explore

This section gives you a chance to investigate the topic in more depth and to make links with other subjects. You may be asked to write about something or do some research.

Ten top tips for working with word problems

1 *Work step-by-step.* Follow the flow chart.

Rain	**Read** the question, now read it again.
Drops	**Decide** your operations and units.
Are	**Approximate** your answer.
Crystal	**Calculate**.
Clear	**Check**.

2 Always *show your working* or 'method'. This will help you to keep track of what you have done and may help you to get extra marks.

3 Always *include the units* in your answer. If you don't, you won't get full marks.

4 When you first read through a question, *underline important words and numbers*. This will help you to remember the important bits.

5 *Draw a picture to help you.* Sometimes a question is easier if you can 'see' it. For example, drawing 6 apples can help you if you need to divide them.

6 If the problem has a number of steps, break it down and do *one step at a time*.

7 To *check your answers*, look at the inverse operation.

8 Sometimes an answer will 'sound right'. Read it out (quietly) and listen. *Does it make sense?*

9 If you are using measurements (grams, litres, cm), make sure that the *units are the same* before you calculate.

10 Once again! *Read the question again and check that your solution answers it.*

Practical problems

Practical problems often involve sorting or arranging objects, cards or numbers in different ways. You may need to make given totals or differences. Some questions may have more than one answer.

Sort these cards into two groups so that each group has the total 10.

 6   **7**   **2**   **1**   **4**

Read the question, now read it again.	Read slowly and carefully. What are you being asked to do?
Decide your operations and units.	I need to add the numbers to make totals of 10.
Approximate your answer.	Which numbers add to make 10? Is there more than one way?
Calculate.	2 + 1 + 7 = 10 and 6 + 4 = 10.
Check.	I can add the numbers in a different order to check, 7 + 1 + 2 = 10 and 4 + 6 = 10. Yes, I am correct!

Hints and tips

Read carefully to see if the question asks for a *total* (adding) or for a *difference* (taking away). Also, think about whether there is more than one possible answer.

Questions

1 a) Arrange the numbers 1 to 5 into the diagram so that each line has a total of 8.

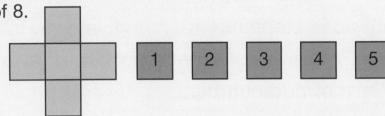

b) Put the same numbers into the diagram so that each line has a total of 9.

c) Put the same numbers into the diagram so that each line has a total of 10.

2 a) Sort the numbers in the circles into pairs so that each pair has a difference of 2.

b) Arrange the numbers in the circles into two groups so that each group has a total of 16.

CHALLENGE

Copy this diagram. Arrange the numbers 1 to 6 in different ways so that each side of the triangle has the same total. How many different solutions can you find?

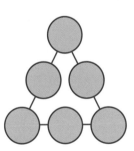

Explore

An artist is designing a square logo made from four small square tiles. There are four tiles; red, yellow, blue and green. Draw some different designs they could make, such as these. Find as many different answers as you can.

Patterns and sequences

Number sequences can go up or down in equal sized steps, such as in steps of one, two, five or ten. When jumping in steps of two you will get a pattern of even numbers or a pattern of odd numbers.

Jo writes a sequence starting with the number 7 and counting on in twos. What is the 8th number in her sequence?

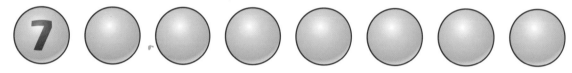

Read the question, now read it again.

Read slowly and carefully. What must you do?

⬇

Decide your operations and units.

I need to count on in twos from 7 to make a sequence.

⬇

Approximate your answer.

The sequence will be all odd numbers, so the answer will be odd.

⬇

Calculate.

7,   9,   11, 13, 15, 17, 19, 21 …
1st 2nd 3rd 4th 5th 6th 7th 8th
The eighth number is 21.

⬇

Check.

I can count back in twos from 21 to see if I can reach 7. Yes, I was correct!

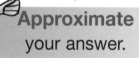

Hints and tips

- Even numbers all end in 2, 4, 6, 8 or 0.
- Odd numbers all end in 1, 3, 5, 7 or 9.

Questions

1

a) How many even numbers lie between 11 and 23?
    What are the numbers?

b) Sam starts with the number 20 and counts on in fives.
    What is the 6th number in the sequence?

c) What are the next three numbers in this sequence?
    8   10   12   14   16   ?   ?   ?

2

a) What is the next number in this sequence?
    2   7   12   17   22   ?

b) The three consecutive odd numbers 3, 5 and 7 have
    a sum of 15.
    Find three consecutive odd numbers with a sum of 27.

c) The three consecutive even numbers 6, 8 and 10 have
    a sum of 24.
    Find three consecutive even numbers with a sum of 42.

CHALLENGE!

Four different odd numbers that are less
than 15 have a total of 36. What could the
four odd numbers be? Find as many
different answers as you can.

Explore

Find some examples to help show whether each of
these statements is **True** or **False**.

- If you add two odd numbers the answer is even.
- If you add two even numbers the answer is odd.
- If you count on in tens from 7, the unit digit of each number will
  always be 7.

Addition and subtraction

For many word questions you find answers by adding or subtracting. Use the number facts that you know to help you or use mental methods to work out the answer.

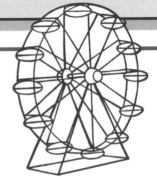

There are 32 capsules on the London Eye. If 19 of the capsules are empty, how many capsules are not empty?

Read the question, now read it again.	Read slowly and carefully. What are you being asked to do?
Decide your operations and units.	I need to take 19 from 32. That is subtracting.
Approximate your answer.	32 – 19 is about 32 – 20 = 12 so the answer will be near to 12.
Calculate.	32 – 19 = 32 – 20 + 1 = 13
Check.	I can add 19 and 13 to see if I get 32. Yes, I was correct!

Hints and tips

When checking an addition, try taking away one of the numbers from your answer to see if you get the other number. When checking a subtraction, add the second number in the question to your answer to see if you get the first number.
For example, for 10 – 3 = 7, add 3 to 7 to check it is 10.

Questions

1

a) There were 14 people in a capsule, then 9 more people got in. How many people are there in the capsule now?

b) There were 23 people in a capsule, then 8 people got out. How many people are there in the capsule now?

c) A capsule can hold 25 people. If there are 7 people in one of the capsules, how many more people can it hold?

2

a) There were 8 people in a capsule, then 9 more people got in and 11 got out. How many people are now in the capsule?

b) An adult ticket costs £18, a senior ticket costs £14 and a child's ticket costs £9. How much will it cost for a small boy, his mother and his grandfather?

c) Mrs Patel buys a child's ticket (£9) and an adult ticket (£18). How much change does she get from £30 ?

CHALLENGE! Imagine a small wheel with five capsules. Each capsule can hold up to 6 people. How many different ways can 25 people fit in to the capsules? One way is shown here. Find as many different ways as you can.

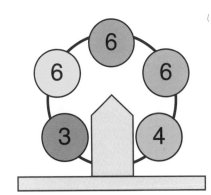

Explore

Go to www.londoneye.com and find out the prices of other tickets or read the *Interesting Facts*. Make up three questions of your own about the London Eye that involve adding or subtracting for a partner to solve.

Doubling and halving

Some word problems involve doubling and halving. Doubling is the opposite of halving. **Doubling** is making something twice as large or multiplying by two and **halving** is splitting it into two halves.

Skye has half as many grapes as her brother Ben. If Skye has 8 grapes, how many does Ben have?

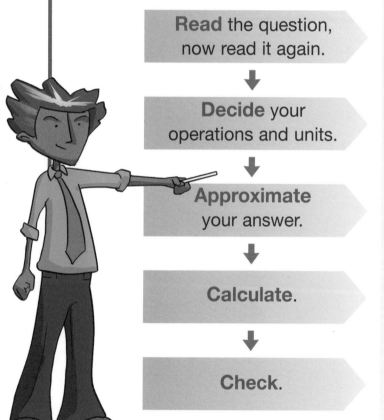

Read the question, now read it again.

⬇

Decide your operations and units.

⬇

Approximate your answer.

⬇

Calculate.

⬇

Check.

Read slowly and carefully. It might say 'half', but sometimes you have to double to find the answer!

Skye has 'half' as many as Ben, but we need to find how many **Ben** has, so I must **double**.

Double 8 is less than double 10, so it will be less than 20.

$8 \times 2 = 16$, so the answer is 16 grapes.

I think Ben has 16 so Skye would have half of 16 which is 8.

Hints and tips

Read the question carefully and think about it before deciding whether to double or halve. Sometimes the question may use the word *double* or *halve* when you must actually do the opposite to find the answer.

Questions

 1 a) James is double Kyle's age. Kyle is 6 years old. How old is James?

b) Mr Larson wins £100. He gives half of the money to his daughter. How much does she get?

2 a) Jo has twice as many cherries as Lee. If Jo has 6 cherries, how many does Lee have?

b) In a field there are 16 sheep, some cows and some horses. If there are twice as many cows as sheep and half as many horses as sheep, how many cows and how many horses are there?

CHALLENGE! Use these clues to work out how heavy each fruit in the list is.
- The grapefruit is twice as heavy as the banana.
- The grape is half the mass of the apricot.
- The melon is double the mass of the grapefruit.
- The apricot is half the mass of the banana.

Melon	___ g
Grapefruit	___ g
Banana	___ g
Apricot	50 g
Grape	___ g

Explore

Are each of these statements **True** or **False**?
- If I double a number, and then double the answer, it is the same as multiplying by 4.
- If I halve a number, and then halve the answer, it is the same as dividing by 4.

Give some examples and make up some questions of your own where you could use this.

Multiplication and division

Sometimes questions are about multiplying, grouping or sharing, where you need to times or divide to find the answer.

Jim's Grandad shares £36 equally between his four grandchildren. How much does he give to each of his grandchildren?

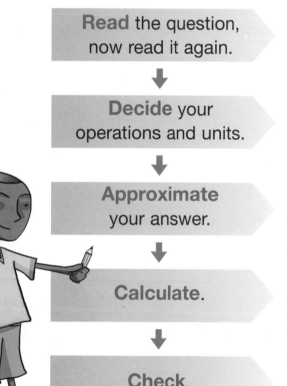

Read the question, now read it again.

Read slowly and carefully. What are you being asked to do?

Decide your operations and units.

I need to share £36 between 4. That is dividing.

Approximate your answer.

I know that £40 divided by 4 is 10 so it will be a bit less than £10.

Calculate.

£36 ÷ 4 = £9

Check.

I can multiply my answer £9 by 4. Yes, that is £36, so I was correct!

Hints and tips

• Use the times tables that you know to help you work out answers to multiplication and division questions.

• Remember that multiplication and division are opposites.

Questions

1 a) For a sponsored walk, Sara raises £4 for each mile she walks. She walks for 5 miles. How much money does she raise?

b) Clare also walks 5 miles. She raises £45. How much does she raise for each mile she walked?

c) The vet gives Sally's dog some pills. The dog needs to have three pills each day. The vet gives Sally 18 pills. How many days will they last?

2 a) I have six 5p coins and four 10p coins. How much money is this?

b) A packet holds 100 seeds. Jim's Grandad plants the seeds in 4 rows. How many seeds are there in each row?

c) I think of a number and divide it by 3. The answer is 9. What was my number?

CHALLENGE!

Grandad wants to plant 48 leeks in equal rows. How many different ways can he do this?

Explore

This table lists the colours of some of the Royal Mail stamps.

1p	Maroon
2p	Dark green
5p	Ash pink
9p	Orange
10p	Light tan
20p	Light green

Kevin buys 12 stamps that are two different colours. Which stamps could he have bought and how much might it have cost him? Find out about other stamps at **www.royalmail.com**.

Mixed calculations

It is important to be able to work out whether to add, subtract, multiply or divide to find the answer to a word problem.

In the school vegetable garden there are 3 rows of carrots, with 8 carrots in each row. If 7 carrots are picked to eat, how many are left?

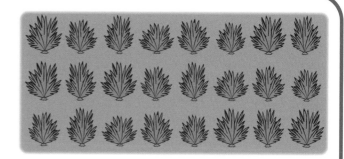

Read the question, now read it again.

Read slowly and carefully. What are you being asked to do?

Decide your operations and units.

I need to find 3 lots of 8. Then I must subtract 7.

Approximate your answer.

Nearly a whole row of carrots is eaten, so the answer will be about 2 lots of 8 which is 16.

Calculate.

$3 \times 8 = 24$
$24 - 7 = 24 - 4 - 3 = 20 - 3 = 17$
17 carrots are left.

Check.

I'll add 7 to 17 to get 24 and I know $3 \times 8 = 24$, so I am correct!

Hints and tips

Some questions will have just one step and others may have more. Think carefully about what to do and read the question carefully to the end.

Questions

1 a) Claire is planting 24 seeds. She puts 6 seeds in each row. How many rows will she plant?

b) Sam picks 10 broad bean pods. In each pod there are 6 beans. How many beans are there altogether?

2 a) Ellie picks 4 onions and 1 cabbage. Each onion weighs 150 g and the cabbage weighs 400 g. How much do the five vegetables weigh altogether?

b) There are 100 seeds in a packet. Alisha plants half of the seeds into two equal rows. How many seeds are in each row?

c) Aiden has 24 tomatoes on a plant. He picks half of them on Monday and he picks five of them on Tuesday. How many tomatoes are left on the plant?

CHALLENGE!

There are some other vegetables in the school garden:

- 12 lettuces
- 9 beetroots
- 6 cauliflowers
- 40 pea pods each with 5 peas inside.

Write three questions of your own about these vegetables for a partner to solve.

Explore

Weigh some fruit or vegetables or find out the prices of them from a greengrocers or an online supermarket. Find out how heavy an apple or potato is or the cost of 1 kg of strawberries or other fruits. Write an information sheet about what you have found out.

Fractions

Some questions are about finding halves and quarters of shapes, numbers or sets of objects.

Ahmed cuts three pizzas into quarters. He shares the pieces equally between six people. How many pieces of pizza does each person get?

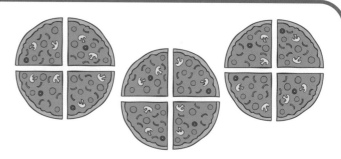

 Read the question, now read it again.

Decide your operations and units.

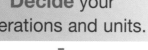 **Approximate** your answer.

Calculate.

Check.

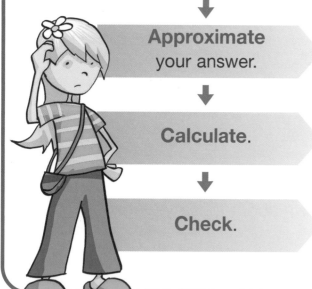

Read slowly and carefully. What are the important numbers?

Each pizza is cut into 4 slices (quarters). There are 3 pizzas. I must then share them between 6 people.

If there are 6 people and 3 pizzas they should each get about half a pizza, which is two of the quarter slices.

$3 \times 4 = 12$ and $12 \div 6 = 2$ so the answer must be 2 pieces each.

6×2 slices = 12 slices. Each slice is a quarter, 12 slices is 3 whole pizzas, so I am correct!

Hints and tips

- A half ($\frac{1}{2}$) means something has been split into two equal parts.
- A quarter ($\frac{1}{4}$) means it has been split into four equal parts.

Questions

1
a) A basket holds 12 slices of garlic bread. Half of them are eaten. How many are not eaten?

b) There are eight olives on Li's pizza. Li eats one-quarter of them. How many olives does she leave?

c) Five pizzas are cut into quarters. How many quarters are there altogether?

2
a) A large pizza is cut into 20 slices. Three-quarters of the slices have ham on and one-quarter of the slices do not have ham on them. How many slices have ham on them?

b) Normally, a large pizza costs £9 and a small costs £6. But all pizzas are now half price. How much will it cost for 2 large pizzas and a small pizza in the sale?

C H A L L E N G E !

Is each of these statements **True** or **False**?
- Half of one half is a quarter.
- One-quarter and three-quarters together make one whole.
- Two-quarters and one-half together make one whole.
- Four-quarters together make two wholes.

Explore

Write a short report about how halves and quarters are used when telling the time. Include some questions and answers like this one: *What time is three-quarters of an hour after seven fifteen?*

Place value and ordering

When solving place value problems it is important to know the value of each digit in a number. The number 284 has 2 hundreds, 8 tens and 4 ones and is smaller than 482 which has 4 hundreds, 8 tens and 2 ones.

In the long jump Chloe jumps 109 cm and Fred jumps 190 cm. Who jumps further and by how much?

Read the question, now read it again.

I need to know whether 109 is larger or smaller than 190.

Decide your operations and units.

I think that 190 is larger than 109, so now I must do 190 take away 109.

Approximate your answer.

This will be about 190 – 100, so the answer will be about 90.

Calculate.

$190 - 109 = 190 - 100 - 9 = 90 - 9 = 81$, so Fred jumps 81 cm further.

Check.

$109 + 81 = 109 + 80 + 1 = 189 + 1 = 190$. Yes, I was correct!

Hints and tips

When comparing and ordering you can arrange numbers in columns to help you. Start by comparing the hundreds digits (H), then the tens digit (T) and finally the units or ones digits (U).

H	T	U
1	9	0
1	0	9
9	0	1

Questions

1 a) Earle throws the javelin five times. These are his results.

65 m   60 m   56 m   67 m   57 m

Put the measurements in order, starting with the **smallest**.

b) Chuck throws the discus six times. These are his results.

70 m   67 m   76 m   66 m   60 m   77 m

Put the measurements in order, starting with the **largest**.

c) In the high jump Sally jumps 198 cm and Joel jumps 189 cm. Who jumps higher and by how much?

2 a) Candy and Andy compare their high jump measurements. Use the < and > signs to show which measurement in each pair is higher. For example, 77 cm > 69 cm.

87 cm 78 cm   95 cm 99 cm   105 cm 110 cm

b) Put these long jump measurements in order, starting with **smallest**.

270 m   207 m   206 m   217 m   260 m   177 m   210 m

CHALLENGE! Use the digits 1, 3 and 6 to make as many different 3-digit numbers as you can (there are six). Put them in order of size, starting with the smallest.

Explore

Find out about some world records in athletics and sports by looking at www.guinnessworldrecords.com. You could even time yourself at some of the events, such as how long it takes you to run 100 m, and compare your own measurements with those of the world record holders.

Money

In questions about money you may need to find the totals of coins and work out change.

Mrs Shaw is putting some coins into a car park ticket machine. She puts in three 10p coins, two 5p coins and a 2p coin. How much did she pay?

 Read the question, now read it again.

Read slowly and carefully. What do you need to do?

 Decide your operations and units.

I need to add three 10p coins, two 5p coins and a 2p coin.

 Approximate your answer.

Three 10p coins are 30p and two 5p coins make 10p so it will be a bit more than 40p.

Calculate.

$3 \times 10p = 30p$, $2 \times 5p = 10p$, $1 \times 2p = 2p$
$30p + 10p + 2p = 42p$

 Check.

I can add in a different order: $2p + 30p + 10p = 42p$

Hints and tips

- These are all the coins used in the United Kingdom: 1p, 2p, 5p, 10p, 20p, 50p, £1 and £2.

- Remember that £1 (one pound) is worth the same as 100p and that ten 10p coins have the same value as £1.

Questions

1 a) Helen has a £1 coin, two 10p coins and three 2p coins. How much does she have in total?

b) Jo puts seven 5p coins into the ticket machine. How much does she pay?

c) Gina must pay 45p for parking. She finds three 5p coins and a 10p coin in her purse. She needs one more coin. Which coin does she need?

2 a) Mr Smith needs to pay 77p for the car park. He pays it with exactly 4 coins. What coins did he pay with?

b) Helen has four 10p coins, a 50p coin and a 2p coin. How much money will she have left after paying 30p for her ticket?

CHALLENGE! This list shows the prices for a car park. Write three questions of your own about people parking and the coins they would need to use to pay. Give the start and end times of the driver's visit to make your questions more difficult.

P Pay here — Car park prices

Up to one hour	45p
One to two hours	60p
Two to four hours	£1

Explore

Investigate these problems:

• Which amounts between 10p and 30p can be made using exactly three coins?

• Find as many different ways as you can to make 29p using different coins.

Number lines

Some problems can be solved by drawing a number line to help you add or subtract. Count forwards or backwards in hundreds, tens or ones to help you find the answer.

Chelsea uses this line to find the difference between 249 and 385. What answer should she give?

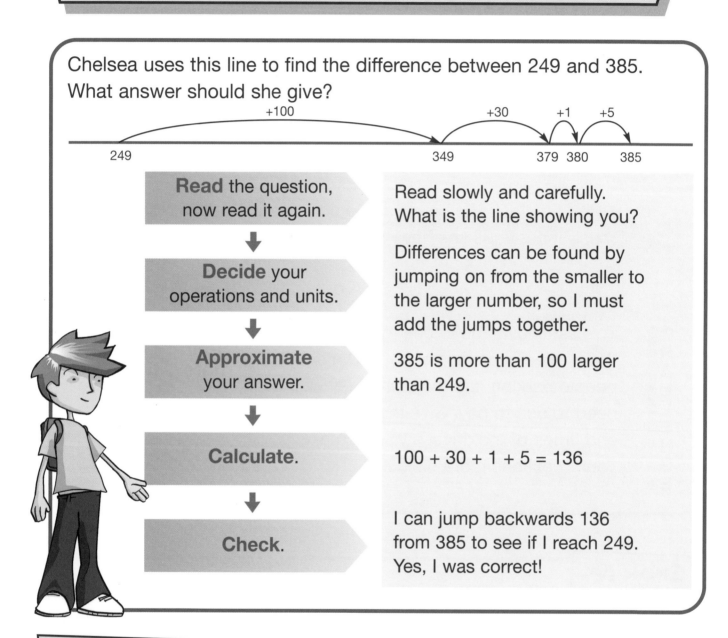

Read the question, now read it again.	Read slowly and carefully. What is the line showing you?
Decide your operations and units.	Differences can be found by jumping on from the smaller to the larger number, so I must add the jumps together.
Approximate your answer.	385 is more than 100 larger than 249.
Calculate.	100 + 30 + 1 + 5 = 136
Check.	I can jump backwards 136 from 385 to see if I reach 249. Yes, I was correct!

Hints and tips

Remember that addition and subtraction are inverses, so you can check an addition by subtracting or a subtraction by adding. Sometimes a number line can be used to show an addition or a subtraction.

Questions

1 a) Ravi adds 49 and 36 together, using this number line. What answer should she give?

+1   +30   +5
49

b) Jason takes 45 from 82 using this number line. What answer should he give?

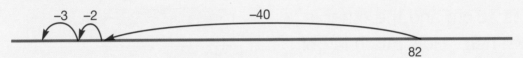

−3 −2   −40
82

2 a) Deepa takes 49 from 173 using this number line. What answer should she give?

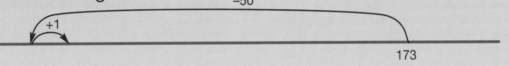

−50
+1
173

b) Use this number line to find the difference between 168 and 207.

168   207

CHALLENGE.

Draw three number lines to show different ways you can find the difference between 27 and 42.

Explore

Look at the numbers on a thermometer and find out about the weather in different parts of the world.

• What is the hottest place in the world?
• What is the coldest place?
• Find the differences between temperatures in different countries.

Measures – length

For questions about length you may need to read the length from a ruler or scale and then add, subtract, multiply or divide.

Ed finds two centipedes. One is 13 cm and the other is shown here. How much larger is one than the other?

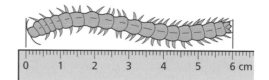

Read the question, now read it again.	Read slowly and carefully. What are you being asked to do?
Decide your operations and units.	I need to subtract the length of the centipede from 13 cm.
Approximate your answer.	The centipede is about 6 cm long. I know that 12 – 6 = 6, so the answer will be close to 6 cm.
Calculate.	13 cm – 6 cm = 7 cm
Check.	I can count on 7 from 6 to get 13. So 13 cm is the right answer!

Hints and tips

Read scales on rulers carefully and remember that 10 millimetres (10 mm) is the same as 1 centimetre (1 cm).

Questions

1 a) If six identical worms, like this one, were put end-to-end without any gaps, how long would the line be?

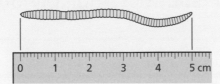

   b) The worm shown above grew an extra 8 cm. What was its final length? Give your answer in millimetres.

2 a) What is the difference in length between the worm shown above and this wasp? Give your answer in millimetres.

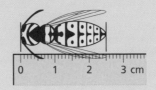

   b) A caterpillar is 38 mm long. An earwig is 47 mm long. What is the difference between their lengths?

   c) From the floor, a spider climbs 38 cm up a wall. It then climbs 17 cm higher before dropping 26 cm. How far from the floor is the spider now?

CHALLENGE!

If I have several sticks that are 2 cm and 5 cm long, what different lengths can I measure with the sticks?

Explore

Find out about the heights of dinosaurs and compare them. Go to www.dinosaur-facts.com or to other websites to find more information.

Measures – capacity

When solving capacity problems you may need to read a scale and then add, subtract, multiply or divide.

A wizard pours some magic potion into this jug. He wants to use one litre of the potion. How much more does he need?

Read the question, now read it again.	How much is a litre? It is the same as 1000 ml.

| Decide your operations and units. | I need to read the scale and subtract the reading from 1000. |

| Approximate your answer. | The scale shows less than 500 ml so the answer will be less than 1000 – 500 = 500 ml. |

| Calculate. | The scale shows 400 ml. 1000 ml – 400 ml = 600 ml |

| Check. | I can add 400 ml and 600 ml to see if it is one litre. It is! |

Hints and tips

Remember that 1000 millilitres (1000 ml) is the same as one litre (1 l).

Questions

1

a) How much magic potion is in this tube?

b) The wizard pours an extra 22 ml into the tube. How much is in there now?

c) The wizard takes 45 ml of potion and pours it equally into five small dishes. How much is in each dish?

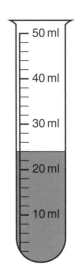

2

a) A jug holds 500 ml of potion and a cup holds 300 ml. The potion from the jug and the cup is poured into a litre bowl. How much more potion is needed to fill the litre bowl?

b) For a spell, the wizard needs one quarter of the potion in this container. How many millilitres does he need?

CHALLENGE!

'The wizard has a large bowl. He puts ___ ml of potion in, takes ___ ml out and then uses half of the potion for a spell. How much is left in the bowl?' Write three questions of your own like this filling in the blanks with numbers.

Explore

A Greek mathematician and scientist called Archimedes made many discoveries about water and liquids, but he is most famously remembered as having jumped out of a bath and shouted 'Eureka!'. Find out more about Archimedes and his discoveries. Make an information sheet about your findings.

Measures – mass

Questions about mass are about how heavy something is, such as 100 g or 24 kg. We use different types of scales to weigh things, such as bathroom or kitchen scales.

A chef has a bowl that weighs 100 g. He puts 150 g of flour and some butter into it. He puts the bowl and ingredients onto these scales. How much butter does he put in?

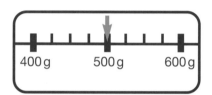

| 400 g | 500 g | 600 g |

Read the question, now read it again.

Read slowly and carefully. What are you being asked to do?

Decide your operations and units.

The bowl and flour weigh 100 g + 150 g. How much more is 500g?

Approximate your answer.

I think the answer will be about 250 g.

Calculate.

$100 + 150 = 250$, $500 - 250 = 250$, so the answer is 250 g.

Check.

I can add 100 g, 150 g and 250 g to check it is 500 g. I was correct!

Hints and tips

Remember that 1000 grams (1000 g) is the same as one kilogram (1 kg).

Questions

1

a) A spoon holds 25 g of flour. A chef puts 5 spoonfuls of flour into a bowl. How many grams of flour is this?

b) How many spoonfuls of flour would be needed to make 250 g of flour?

2

a) This scale shows the mass of two identical apples. How heavy is each apple?

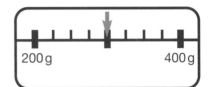

200 g   400 g

b) Kim has five apples like these. What is their total mass?

c) What is the mass of half of one of these apples?

CHALLENGE!

Luke has a set of balance scales, but only has 3 kg and 4 kg weights. What masses up to 20 kg can he measure with these weights?

Clue: weights can be in both pans of the scales.

Explore

There are many different types of weighing scales. With a partner, find out about the different types and what they are used for. What is a spring scale or a weigh bridge? How are small things weighed? What about lorries and cars? What numbers are used on the scales? Make a leaflet from your findings.

Time

To solve time problems you need to be able to read the time on a clock face (analogue clock) and on a digital clock.

This clock shows the time that a TV cartoon starts.
The cartoon finishes at **quarter to** four.
How many minutes long is it?

Read the question, now read it again.

Read carefully and look at the clock. What do you need to do?

Decide your operations and units.

The clock shows 'half past three'. How many minutes until 'quarter to four'? I must count on to that time.

Approximate your answer.

'Half past three' is 3:30 and 'quarter to four' is 3:45 which is quarter of an hour apart.

Calculate.

Counting on in fives.

3:30 3:35 3:40 3:45

Check.

I can count back 15 minutes from quarter to four to half past three to make sure.

Hints and tips

There are 60 minutes in a whole hour, 30 minutes in half an hour and 15 minutes in a quarter of an hour.
Remember that for digital times the hour is written first, so 4:15 is 'quarter past four'.

Questions

 1 a) A talent show starts at **six o'clock**.
It finishes at the time shown on this clock.
How many hours long is the show?

b) A quiz show lasts for **half an hour**. It starts at **3:45**.
What time does it end? Write your answer in digital time.

c) A nature programme starts at 8 o'clock and finishes at 8:45.
How long is the programme?

2 a) The digital clocks show the start and
end times of a film. How long is the film in
hours and minutes?

b) What is the length of the film in minutes?

c) A game show lasts for 45 minutes. It finishes at 7:30.
What time did it start?

CHALLENGE! Look at a TV guide and write down the times of different programmes. Make up three questions of your own about how long each programme lasts.

Explore

Find out about different clocks and watches and other ways of telling the time. What is an hour glass? Why did people used to use them? How do sun dials work? How does a water clock work? Draw some pictures of different ways of telling the time.

2-D and 3-D shapes

When solving shape problems you need to remember the names of common shapes and their properties, such as how many sides, faces or angles they have.

Raz is drawing pentagons onto dotty grids. He counts the number of right angles in each pentagon and finds the total. What is his total?

a	b	c	d	e	f

Read the question, now read it again.

Read slowly and carefully. What are you being asked to do?

Decide your operations and units.

I need to look at each shape and count the number of right angles in each and then add them.

Approximate your answer.

There are six shapes. If each shape had two right angles that would be 12 right angles in total.

Calculate.

$3 + 0 + 2 + 1 + 3 + 2$
$= 11$ right angles.

Check.

I will count them up again.
Yes, I was correct!

Hints and tips

A right angle is a quarter turn. To check for right angles, tear a small corner off a piece of paper and see if it fits onto the edges of the shape.

Questions

1 a) What is the total number of sides of a square, a triangle and a hexagon?

b) A cube has eight vertices (corners). How many vertices do four cubes have altogether?

c) One of these shapes is a symmetrical octagon. Which shape is it?

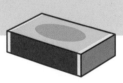

2 a) Faye draws a shape with two lines of symmetry. The shape has four right angles and four straight sides. What is the name of the shape she has drawn?

b) Adam picks up a plastic pyramid. It has five faces and one of them is square. What shape are the four other faces?

c) Chloe has some objects on the table. She is asked to pick up a cylinder. Which of these objects should she pick up?

    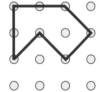

CHALLENGE!

How many different hexagons can be drawn on a 4 × 4 pinboard? Explain how many lines of symmetry and how many right angles each hexagon has.

Explore

Draw some patterns and designs made from triangles, rectangles and other shapes. Look out for shapes in patterns on wrapping paper, wallpaper, bags, curtains and other types of material. Copy any interesting designs and write what shapes you can see.

Position and direction

When solving problems about position and direction you may be asked to give or follow a set of instructions, such as turning through a right angle and moving two steps forward.

If James follows these instructions which letter does he reach?

- Move forward onto the red square.
- Move forward two squares.
- Turn a quarter turn to the left.
- Move forward three squares.
- Turn a quarter turn to the right.
- Move forward five squares.

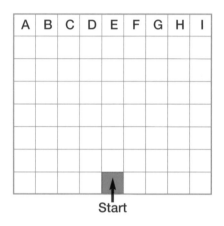

Start

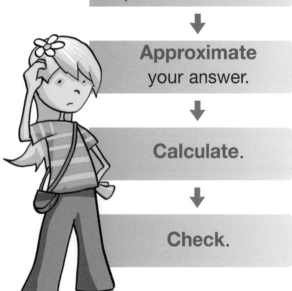

Read the question, now read it again.	Read slowly and carefully. What are you being asked to do?
Decide your operations and units.	I need to follow the instructions carefully.
Approximate your answer.	The first turn is to the left, so I think it will be one of the left-hand letters.
Calculate.	I follow the instructions on the grid and reach B.
Check.	I can work backwards, doing the opposite each time to see if I reach the start. Yes, I was correct!

Hints and tips

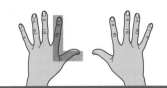

Make sure you know your left and your right! One way to help you remember is to hold your palms away from you, like this. Your **LEFT** hand makes an **L** shape.

Questions

1 Follow these instructions.
Which letter do you reach?
- Move forward onto the red square.
- Turn a quarter turn to the right.
- Move forward four squares.
- Turn a quarter turn to the left.
- Move forward seven squares.

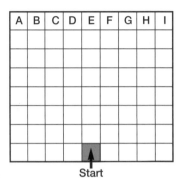

2 a) Write a set of instructions for the yellow route through the grid.

b) Write a set of instructions for the green route through the grid.

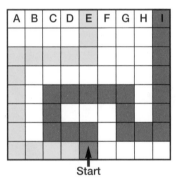

CHALLENGE.

Write a set of instructions to help someone move through this maze or draw one of your own on squared paper and write instructions for a partner to follow.

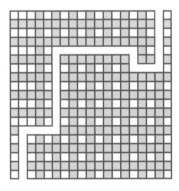

Explore

People have always been fascinated by mazes and labyrinths. Find out more about them online or design your own on squared paper or using a website such as:
http://gwydir.demon.co.uk/jo/maze/makemaze/index.htm.

Tables

Make sure that you understand what information is shown in a list or table. For this type of problem you need to work out which numbers are important and sometimes find totals or differences.

This table shows the number of different birds seen on a bird table on **Monday**. How many birds were seen altogether?

Bird	Number
Robin	2
Blackbird	5
Sparrow	7
Chaffinch	4
Wren	1

 Read the question, now read it again.

Look at the numbers in the table. What do you need to do?

 Decide your operations and units.

I need to find the total of all the numbers of birds.

 Approximate your answer.

There are five small numbers, so I think the answer will be less than 25.

 Calculate.

$2 + 5 + 7 + 4 + 1 = 7 + 7 + 5$
$= 14 + 5 = 19$ birds

Check.

I can add the numbers in a different order to make sure.

Hints and tips

Look at the headings of the table first. They will tell you what the information is trying to show.

Questions

1 a) Look at the table opposite. How many more blackbirds were seen than wrens on Monday?

b) How many more sparrows than robins were seen on Monday?

This table shows the number of birds seen on Tuesday. Compare the two tables.

Bird	Number
Robin	3
Blackbird	7
Sparrow	3
Chaffinch	9
Wren	0

2 a) How many more sparrows were seen on Monday than on Tuesday?

b) What was the total number of birds seen on Tuesday?

c) How many more birds were seen on Tuesday than on Monday?

CHALLENGE! On Wednesday only 15 birds altogether were seen on the bird table. Draw your own table and write how many of each bird might have been seen. Then write some questions of your own about the information.

Explore

Do your own bird table survey and draw a table to show how many birds you have seen.

Graphs, charts and diagrams

Data-handling questions will ask you to look at a graph, a chart or a diagram and use the data to answer questions.

Here is a bar chart showing the number of different animals brought into a vet's surgery one morning.

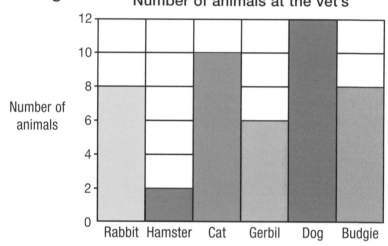

Number of animals at the vet's

How many more dogs were brought into the vet's than hamsters?

Read the question, now read it again.

Read slowly and carefully. What are you being asked to do?

Decide your operations and units.

The bar chart is telling me how many of each type of pet were taken to the vet's.

Approximate your answer.

I have to look at all the information given to me.

Calculate.

There were 12 dogs brought in and only 2 hamsters. This is a difference of 10.

Check.

I can add 10 to 2 and check I get 12. Yes, I was correct!

Hints and tips

- Look at the title of the graph and read the scale carefully.
- They will tell you what the information is trying to show.
- The scale on this graph goes up in twos.

Questions

1 a)   How many cats were brought in?

b)   How many more rabbits than gerbils were brought in?

c)   There were the same number of rabbits as which other animal?

d)   Which was the most common pet brought in?

2 a)   How many animals were brought in altogether?

b)   In the afternoon 50 animals were brought in. How many more is this than in the morning?

CHALLENGE.   Do your own survey about what pets people have. Collect the data in a table and then draw your own bar chart on squared paper. Write some questions about the data in your bar chart for a partner to answer.

Explore

Look online, in magazines or newspapers for examples of bar charts. Can you work out what they are trying to show?

Answers

Practical problems
(Pages 10–11)
Questions:
1 a) Example answer:

```
      4
  5 | 1 | 2
      3
```

b) Example answer:

```
      4
  5 | 3 | 1
      2
```

c) Example answer:

```
      4
  3 | 5 | 2
      1
```

2 a) 8, 6; 7, 5; 4, 2
   b) 8, 6, 2; 7, 5, 4
Challenge:
Totals such as 9 and 12 can be made, e.g.

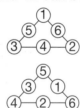

Explore:
There are 24 different solutions, although some are rotations or reflections of each other.

Patterns and sequences
(Pages 12–13)
Questions:
1 a) 6; 12, 14, 16, 18, 20, 22
   b) 45
   c) 18, 20, 22
2 a) 27
   b) 7, 9, 11
   c) 12, 14, 16
Challenge:
There are two solutions, 3, 9, 11, 13 or 5, 7, 11, 13.
Explore:
True, False, True, True.

Addition and subtraction
(Pages 14–15)
Questions:
1 a) 23
   b) 15
   c) 18
2 a) 6
   b) £41
   c) £3
Challenge:
There are seven solutions if order is not taken into account:
1, 6, 6, 6, 6
2, 5, 6, 6, 6
3, 4, 6, 6, 6
3, 5, 5, 6, 6
4, 4, 5, 6, 6
4, 5, 5, 5, 6
5, 5, 5, 5, 5

Doubling and halving
(Pages 16–17)
Questions:
1 a) 12 years old
   b) £50
2 a) 3
   b) 32 cows, 8 horses
Challenge:
Melon 400 g
Grapefruit 200 g
Banana 100 g
Apricot 50 g
Grape 25 g
Explore:
True, True.

Multiplication and division
(Pages 18–19)
Questions:
1 a) £20
   b) £9
   c) 6 days
2 a) 70p
   b) 25 seeds
   c) 27
Challenge:
1 row of 48, 2 rows of 24, 3 rows of 16, 4 rows of 12, 6 rows of 8, 8 rows of 6, 12 rows of 4, 16 rows of 3, 24 rows of 2 and 48 rows of 1.

Mixed calculations
(Pages 20–21)
Questions:
1 a) 4 rows
  b) 60 beans
2 a) 1000 g or 1 kg
  b) 50 seeds
  c) 7 tomatoes

Fractions
(Pages 22–23)
Questions:
1 a) 6 slices
  b) 6 olives
  c) 20 quarters
2 a) 15 slices
  b) £12
Challenge:
True, True, True, False.

Place value and ordering
(Pages 24–25)
Questions:
1 a) 56 m, 57 m, 60 m,
    65 m, 67 m
  b) 77m, 76 m, 70 m,
    67 m, 66 m, 60 m
  c) Sally by 9 cm
2 a) 87 cm>78 cm
    95 cm<99 cm
    105 cm<110 cm
  b) 177 m, 206 m,
    207 m, 210 m,
    260 m, 270 m
Challenge:
136, 163, 316, 361, 613, 631

Money
(Pages 26–27)
Questions:
1 a) £1.26
  b) 35p
  c) 20p
2 a) 50p, 20p, 5p, 2p
  b) 62p

Number lines
(Pages 28–29)
Questions:
1 a) 85
  b) 37
2 a) 124
  b) 39

Measures – length
(Pages 30–31)
Questions:
1 a) 30 cm
  b) 130 mm
2 a) 25 mm
  b) 9 mm
  c) 29 cm
Challenge:
Any length in whole centimetres can be made,
e.g. 5 cm next to two 2 cm sticks will have a
gap of 1 cm etc.

Measures – capacity
(Pages 32–33)
Questions:
1 a) 24 ml
  b) 46 ml
  c) 9 ml
2 a) 200 ml
  b) 15 ml
Challenge:
855 ml

Measures – mass
(Pages 34–35)
Questions:
1 a) 125 g
  b) 10 spoonfuls
2 a) 150 g
  b) 750 g
  c) 75 g
Challenge:
Any mass in whole kilograms can be measured
using the weights in both pans, e.g. 1 kg can be
weighed with 3 kg in one pan and 4 kg in the
other.

Time
(Pages 36–37)
Questions:
1 a) 3 hours
  b) 4:15
  c) 45 minutes or $\frac{3}{4}$ of an hour
2 a) 1 hour 15 minutes
  b) 75 minutes
  c) 6:45

2-D and 3-D shapes
(Pages 38–39)
Questions:
1 a) 13
  b) 32
  c) D
2 a) rectangle
  b) triangles
  c) coin

Position and direction
(Pages 40–41)
Questions:
1 I
2 a)
Move on to red square;
turn a quarter turn to left;
move forward 4 squares;
turn a quarter turn to right;
move forward 5 squares;
turn a quarter turn to right;
move forward 4 squares;
turn a quarter turn to left;
move forward 2 squares.
2 b)
Move on to red square;
move forward 1 square;
turn a quarter turn to left;
move forward 2 squares;
turn a quarter turn to right;
move forward 2 squares;
turn a quarter turn to right;
move forward 4 squares;
turn a quarter turn to right;
move forward 2 squares;
turn a quarter turn to left;
move forward 2 squares;
turn a quarter turn to left;
move forward 6 squares.

Tables
(Pages 42–43)
Questions:
1 a) 4
  b) 5
2 a) 4
  b) 22
  c) 3

Graphs, charts and diagrams
(Pages 44–45)
Questions:
1 a) 10 cats
  b) 2
  c) budgie
  d) dog
2 a) 46
  b) 4